The Kingdom Playlist

A 31 Day Devotional for Christian Millennials

By: Audrey Todd

November Media Publishing

Chicago, IL

November Media Publishing, Chicago IL.

Copyright © **2019 Audrey Todd**

November Media Publishing info@novembermediapublishing.com

Ordering Information: Special discounts are available on quantity purchases by corporations, associations, and others. For details, contact the publisher at the email address above.

Printed in the United States of America

Produced & Published by November Media Publishing

ISBN: 978-1-7337724-8-8 (Print Copy)

Scripture references: KJV Bible, English Standard Version, New International Version, and Gods Word Versions

First Edition : November 2019

10 9 8 7 6 5 4 3 2 1

Table of Context

Dedication

This book is dedicated to my mother, Florence Todd, who gave me the first and final push to birth this book and took the lead in heaven before the completion of this book.

Introduction

Studies show millennials are the largest group of people whose beliefs about God are uncertain. Churches are trying to find common ground and relativity to support this growing group of churchgoers. Many young people, both churched and unchurched, are finding their way to the house of God for more answers. They need direction to get them to their divine purpose ordained by God for their lives. This devotional place emphasis on recognizing who we are in Christ and what he requires of us to bring him glory. This devotional is fully inspired by the Holy Spirit and is intended to inform, encourage, and empower Christian millennials to live a bold, dauntless, and purposeful life before Christ.

Christian millennials are being challenged daily in areas they have not been well equipped to handle. They are challenged to live a life that, to many, may be impossible to live. The media plays a big part in the struggles Christian millennials face, presenting a blurred image of Christians in general, and it can mislead millennials on what is acceptable behavior.

The church is trying to find a way to reach millennials and to bridge the gap between the youth and the church. Some even go so far as to compromise the Word in efforts to make living for Christ appear much easier than it is. Although the delivery method of the Word may change, God is not a progressive God. His statutes and precepts are forever binding and will not change from generation to generation. He does not think as we think; his ways are beyond our ways. He is constant. What he requires will always be good. Living for Christ will require a constrained lifestyle. He requires that we seek his knowledge to enable us to live a pleasing life before him and not depend on the world for direction.

I wish I could tell you the journey would be easy. I wish I could tell you the criticism for following Christ would never come. I wish I could tell you that you won't get discouraged, you'll pass every test, and tribulations will never find you. What I can tell you is that the journey won't be easy, but it will be well worth it.

One thing is for sure, God will never leave you to figure this thing out on your own. It's reassuring to know that a God so big has taken an interest in your destiny and has set you up for a lifetime of blessings and favor. To live a fulfilled pleasing life to him, it will take strengthening your relationship with Christ. There are key principles/values as a Christian millennial that you must pursue and exemplify. These guiding principles will empower you to live your best life in Christ.

DAY 1

Please Identify Yourself

*But ye are a chosen generation, a royal
priesthood, an holy nation, a peculiar people,
that ye should show forth the praises of him
who hath called you out of darkness into his
marvelous light.
(1 Peter 2:9)*

So you've decided to follow Christ... Now what? First off, you have just made the best decision you will make in your lifetime. You've decided to no longer live with the fears of the unknown as you go through life. You've decided to allow the most trustworthy, reliable, faithful person known to mankind to purposefully orchestrate your life. You've decided to do, act, think, and live life to its fullest potential. You've decided to be different, strange, peculiar, an anomaly. You've just decided to no longer conform to societal standards of living, but you've chosen to be a yielded vessel, an instrument to do a mighty work to bring glory to God. Your identity is now a reflection of him who has called you out from darkness to light.

You've decided to advance the kingdom by any means necessary. This means your life has just shifted from ordinary to extraordinary. You've decided to take ownership of all the blessings stored up for you by God. Embrace your new heritage. You are royalty; therefore, you are not bound to a common lifestyle.

Life as you once knew it to be is no more, although society will constantly remind you of the freedom you have to do anything you want. Often, we work hard to create our own persona, and unfortunately, we may end up discouraged, frustrated, and even confused as to who we want to become or be identified as by our peers. The only true way to discover your identity is to build a relationship with the one who made you: God. Recognize that the urge you feel to create your own self-image is really a desire to be who God called you to be. For you were fearfully and wonderfully made in his image. (Psalm 139:14). Your identity now proclaims to the world you are living proof of the power of the Almighty God. Understanding who you are in Christ will give you a strong foundation to build your life on. It is the key to living a purposeful life.

Declaration: I am an identified worshipper.

Prayer: Dear God, I've decided to serve you with every fiber of my being. I understand I am no longer my own but yours. Thank you for my new identity. I commit my ways, thoughts, actions, and lifestyle to you so that others will glorify you for your incomparable power. Continue to do good works in my life forever. Amen!

DAY 2

Understanding My Value

Fear not therefore: ye are of more value than
many sparrows (Matthew 10:31).

Did you know that you are so valuable to God that he was willing to pay the highest price in the universe to redeem you – his only begotten son, Jesus? The world will always challenge your decision to live for Christ. At times, you may even find yourself wondering if the decision was worth it or if you are worth it. God always affirms our value to him and in him. He constantly reminds us of his unfailing love and holds true to all his promises. You are somebody in Christ. You were hand-picked to be a carrier of his glory. This means your value has increased far beyond your imagination. Never again should you allow someone to underestimate your value. You've taken on the only power that enables us to be victorious in all that we do. Your worth is not determined by people or past mistakes. It is determined by who God called you to be before the world was framed. It is based upon all the blessings and rich heritage passed down to you from ages to ages. You are an asset to the kingdom of God and a threat to the enemy's camp. God thought you were worth the investment, so he chose you! Your value will never depreciate.

When we think of the most valuable jewels in the world, we almost instantly think of diamonds and rubies. The more rare and exclusive these gems are, the more value they hold. Consider yourself a rarity, priced far above the common person others may believe you to be. They see you at face value, while God has appraised your worth as far more than that. Because you were chosen by God, man's validation is irrelevant. Once you understand your value in Christ, you will never settle for the norm or a regular life. You will always crave the very best life has to offer because your DNA was formed in Christ. You're so valuable that he has already mapped out your life's story, which further ensures you a successful and prosperous life. Because you were cherry-picked and perfectly crafted by the master craftsman himself, you are constrained to live a life exceeding the societal standards of mere men. You are a child of God, and his Word overwhelmingly boasts that you are his most prized possession.

Declaration: I am an asset to the kingdom of God.

Prayer: Dear God, now that I understand my value, help me to walk in confidence and reflect it in my daily walk. Thank you for paying the highest price for the redemption of my life. Father, I thank you for showing me just how amazing your love for me is. I will no longer focus on past failures but will look forward to being the shining diamond from the rough you have chosen to shed light on in this dark world. I will forever make mention of your name. In Jesus's name, I pray. Amen.

DAY 3

Maintaining My Focus

Let thine eyelids look right on, and let your eyelids look straight before thee (Proverbs 4:25).

This journey you are embarking upon is one that will take commitment and perseverance. To be successful in both, you must keep the main goal in the forefront of everything you do. Why? This will ensure a purpose-filled life. God already has your path and destiny mapped out. He understands there will be obstacles on your path that will cause you to stumble, lose focus, and possibly attempt to revert back to your former, more familiar life. That's why God always promises to deliver us from those roadblocks if we set our focus on him. Wondering how to stay focused? Visualize the results of staying on track and remaining committed to him. Keep the big picture in mind. Your life is not just about you any longer; you now have a generation of unchurched, unlearned, unindoctrinated millennials who are desperately looking for purpose in life. You are someone's kinsman-redeemer, as described in the story of Naomi and Ruth. They will come to know the fullness of Christ by the living example you set before them.

This can also make your journey a tad bit more difficult to endure. Many people cringe at the thought of their life being used as a measurement of how to live life. However, this is a great and rewarding task God had entrusted you with. When your life is on display, it's automatically assumed you should be as close to perfect as humanly possible. Although this is definitely not the case, we still feel pressure to live a better life because of the public attention our lifestyle will receive. You cannot afford to lose sight of your mission. You are an impactor, agent of change, atmosphere-shifter, planet-shaker, and earth-mover. You were equipped to handle the task at hand. Don't be intimidated by the process. You were born victorious. Isaiah 26:3 reminds us that he will keep us in perfect peace as long as our minds are focused on him. We can't let the world distract us. When Peter allowed the wind to distract him, he began to sink, but as long as he gave no attention to his surroundings, he was able to do the impossible: walk on water. You must maintain your focus. Once you lose sight of it, it will be difficult to regain ground. Keep your eyes on God, and he will establish you and keep you from falling.

Declaration: I am committed to maintaining my focus on the task set before me.

Prayer: Heavenly Father, I recognize there is a great assignment before me. Help me never to lose sight of doing good and striving for perfection in you. Keep me on track and focused on the bigger picture. I pray that even my smallest accomplishments will bring you glory and honor. In Jesus's name, I pray. Amen.

DAY 4

Strength Training

God is our refuge and strength, a very present help in trouble. (Psalm 46:1)

It can be so easy to reconsider your vow made to God. With pressure coming from every angle to deter you, it can be easy to submit to fleshly desires. But there is hope for you. You do not have to succumb to this attack from the enemy. We find that in times of weariness and anxiety, God will remain in the struggle with us. Not only will he uplift and protect you, but he will give you strength to endure the challenges you are facing. He understands that for you to live boldly and without compromise, you will need the manpower to keep you going day by day. In the natural sense, strength training is designed to build a stronger heart and improve blood flow, balance, and coordination. Strength training is highly recommended for those seeking to transform their physical appearance. Just as it is naturally, so it is spiritually. You cannot maintain your spiritual balance without spiritual strength training. The way we build our strength in Christ is by enduring situations designed to challenge us. Each situation must be met with tenacity and determination. Your strength can only be built through the process of endurance. Each difficulty you overcome with the strength of God will build your spiritual muscles. Spiritual muscles tell the enemy, "I'm built for any curveball you throw my way." It tells him, "I'm equipped for this journey and well prepared to execute my mission."

The time that you feel most vulnerable to giving up is the best place to be in. Why? Because God's strength is made perfect when you are weak, for his strength can only be granted when you're fragile and weak. It is only when you have humbled yourself and made known to God that you are unable to spiritually withstand the challenges you are facing, that he can step in and take action on your behalf. There will be others to start the journey with you who will quit. Some will compromise. Some will try to stick to the mission, roaming aimlessly about, not knowing the right path to take, leaning and depending on their own knowledge to direct them. Some of your peers will make abrupt decisions, altering God's plans for their lives. Why? Because sometimes it's easier to let go than to continue. No one has ever told them they're not alone and that God will give them the strength to maintain and keep going. There's strength waiting on you in every phase of this walk. Always remember you have the upper hand and you will always triumph.

Declaration: I am strong because that is who you made me to be.

Prayer: God, I thank you. I can rest in knowing I can do all things through you because you have strengthened me. I believe in your power and trust you will build me up in trying times. I take pleasure in knowing I am victorious even in my weakest state. Continue to strengthen me for the journey ahead. In Jesus's name, I pray. Amen.

DAY 5

My Purpose Is My Assignment

*But I have raised you up for this very purpose
and that my name might be proclaimed in all the
earth. (Exodus 9:16)*

On this journey, you will discover that God will lead people on different paths. It's important to remember that although pathways may differ, everyone shares the same common goal and purpose, which is to bring glory to Christ. No matter what your ordained calling is, ultimately, it aligns with the kingdom of God. No one can undo God's purpose for your life. There may be several ways to fulfill the purpose God requires, but he will give concrete instructions on how to accomplish your underlying purpose, which is to bring him honor.

Most times, we tend to believe we have a choice in our purpose. The truth of the matter is that God's purpose for us is more important than any plan we can orchestrate for our lives. As we deepen our relationship with God, he will give us insight regarding our purpose. Making the decision to serve Christ means allowing him to guide your footsteps so that you fulfill your God-designed purpose. Deciding to follow Christ means you've accepted his command to share with others the power of Jesus. As a Christian, one of our most important assignments is to bring others into the knowledge of Christ. Yes, it is an assignment without an expiration date. Our salvation shows an example of the unfailing love shown towards us in spite of not being worthy. To ensure we stick to this assignment, we will have to stay in constant communication (prayer) with God.

Reading his Word will give us clarity and direction to help us avoid the pitfall of abandoning our purpose and assignment. To fulfill our purpose in Christ, we must do things his way because our way will not yield the same results as obeying God's way. We have to be careful in this walk not to get to the point where we believe we have it all figured out. As he leads us, that's how we should follow. We don't have the credentials to search his understanding. Who wouldn't want to exchange a normal life for a more purposeful one? It will all be worth it.

Declaration: I will live a purpose-filled life and complete my God-ordained assignment.

Prayer: God, without you, I am the sum total of nothing. I desire to know my purpose so that I may fulfill it and bring you glory. Give me an unquenchable thirst to only desire what you desire for me. I thank you for entrusting me with this assignment, and I pray I will always bring glory to your kingdom. In Jesus's name, I pray. Amen.

DAY 6

Stay Woke

Be sober, be vigilant, because your adversary the devil, as a roaring lion walketh about, seeking whom he may devour. (1 Peter 5:8)

The enemy is out to distract and deceive every believer. His ultimate goal is to destroy you. He will come in various forms to try to accomplish his mission. You have an assignment, and so does he. He will come in the form of toxic friends, social media, music, and any other avenue he feels may be an effective way to distract you from God's purpose for you. We have to accept the fact that it will never be easy at any point during our journey, but we will become wiser. We can never assume we will arrive at a place where the enemy is no longer after us. As long as we remain in Christ, the enemy will always be present to attempt to get us off course. We must be on guard at all times. He wants to sabotage our destiny by any means necessary. God already knew the struggle you would be up against, so trust that he has already devised your path to escape the tactics of the enemy.

Just because you are young, it does not disqualify you from using Godly wisdom. He gives wisdom freely to those who ask of it. Just ask King Solomon. He asked God to grant him wisdom, and God granted it bountifully. Without the wisdom of God, it will be almost impossible to be vigilant and alert for the enemy's traps. Wisdom will help you discern truth from error. You won't be easily tricked by the world as to what's required of you from God. Godly wisdom will give you spiritual insight into worldly matters, helping you to avoid the enemy's pitfalls. You cannot be spiritually asleep during your walk with God. You have to be woken in spirit, or you will fall prey to Satan's tactics. "Stay woke" in the secular world speaks of the need for awareness and mindfulness on a particular issue within our society. However, this concept of heightened awareness is derived from the Word of God. Staying woke for Christians is the call to be aware of demonic devices whose intent is to destroy us. Thanks be to God, who always causes us to triumph and win! Keep your eyes fixed, but above all else keep them open. Be attentive. Do not hit the snooze button. This is a warning: we are in a spiritual battle. Do not allow the adversary the room to consume you. Stay woke!

Declaration: I have a sound mind, and I will not bow to the tricks of the adversary.

Prayer: Lord, I am aware of the enemy's plan to sift me as wheat, but I thank you that you have already prayed for me.

Help me to discern your perfect will so that I may serve you all the days of my life. Help me to be spiritually attentive at all times. Help me not to be gullible but focused and mindful of traps set by the enemy. I thank you for the knowledge and wisdom that will allow my spiritual journey to be a success. In Jesus's name, I pray. Amen!

DAY 7

Influential and Full of Potential

Ye are the salt of the earth; but if the salt has
lost his savour, where with shall it be salted? It is
thenceforth good for nothing, but to be cast out,
and to be trodden under foot of men.
(Matthew 5:13)

It is important to understand your ability to impact your generation. Believe it or not, your influence on other millennials will be the most meaningful force they encounter. The easiest way to influence someone is to be an example of what it is you are endorsing. Young people influence other young people. The Bible refers to us being the salt because salt is the most dominant of seasonings, and its flavor cannot be contained or overpowered. Compared to other seasonings, it has the greatest impact on food. In fact, it is used in all other seasonings to increase their flavor. That is how powerful salt is. If salt were to lose its flavor, what good would it be, especially if other seasonings rely on it as well? No other seasoning can replace salt; it has its own significance. It is in a class by itself.

Don't allow the enemy to dictate the power of influence you will have on this generation. You are a world-changer, atmosphere-shifter, and influencer.

You are more influential than you can imagine. You are full of potential. You are capable of winning souls for Christ. Someone is waiting on you to show them Christ. Your living example will inspire others to seek God. People are searching for hope, looking for something different in life than what they have become accustomed to. You are that difference. You have been equipped with power that is a magnetic force. Other young people will witness your lifestyle and marvel. You have the responsibility of showing them God. You must understand that every aspect of your life must reflect Christ to effectively influence your peers. You must uphold the standard of righteousness and holiness if you are seeking to convert others. There has to be something different about your way of living versus those who claim to follow Christ but whose lifestyles don't reflect the God they claim to serve. This is not an easy task. In fact, it is one of the most challenging parts of deciding to follow Christ. Once the enemy discovers that you are aware of the potential you have to destroy his kingdom and realizes how powerful your influence is, he will launch an all-out attack to discourage you. This will prevent you from being a successful witness and example. What he doesn't realize is that the power God has placed in you is more powerful than any demonic force. The enemy has already lost. Prove it to him.

Affirmation: I will influence my generation by my living example.

Prayer: Loving God, thank you for entrusting me with my generation. Thank you for giving me the power to positively impact my peers. Help me to never lose my savor but, rather, add it to those who are unaware of your saving power. Teach me how to effectively win souls for you, and may you get the glory of every letter of my name. In Jesus's name, I pray. Amen.

DAY 8

I'm Not Missing Out

Thou wilt show me the path of life: In thy presence is fullness of joy; in thy right hand there are pleasures forevermore. (Psalms 16:11)

Many millennials will refuse to accept Christ because of the fear of missing out on life. Our society tends to capitalize on our fears of missing out. The mass media always gives us reasons to covet material possessions and desire certain lifestyles, and it even has a bearing on deciding what physical characteristics we should want in a partner. All of what you read and observe are false perceptions that the enemy wants to be embedded in your mind, and he has strategically designed them to cause you to falter in your walk with Christ.

The world has determined what fun looks like and urges youth to live life on the edge. Do not get caught up with the false pretenses of how life needs to be lived to enjoy it. God tells us that being in his presence gives us fullness of joy. This means the joy he gives is incomparable and greatly outweighs any other feeling worldly pleasures can ever provide. God wants you to realize your quest of being fulfilled begins, and it ends with him at the center. He can fully satisfy every area of your life.

Feel the pressure to do things you once did before accepting Christ? Ask him to change your desires to reflect his. People will often stress the importance of balance between spiritual and natural things. But you must master distinction first to avoid carnality. Is it possible to live a fulfilled life while being saved and committed to Christ? Absolutely! In fact, you are living your best life if you are saved. Your quality of life increases when you are in Christ. The world's view of an abundant life differs from God's. You chose to follow Christ, so go all in!

The world will boldly represent worldly things with no hesitation. We should be just as charged to represent our God. You have to have the audacity to proclaim, "For God, I live, and for God, I die." This world and the things of it will eventually pass away, but we can rest assured that the kingdom of God will stand forever. Are you in, or are you out?

Declaration: I am living my best life now!

Prayer: Dear God, thank you for confirming just how much joy I can find in you. Help me to realize the importance of seeking after you more than worldly pleasures. I want to be a credible witness to my generation, proving I'm not missing out but enjoying life in Christ. Help others to see you when they observe me and allow my witness to win souls for you. In Jesus's name. Amen.

DAY 9

No Boundaries

It is high as heaven, what canst thou do.
(Job 11:9)

There's a saying: "The sky's the limit." However, in Christ, the sky is not the limit. Being in Christ has many perks and advantages. One is that there are no limitations or boundaries on how you can prosper and excel in life. Age is not a factor when it comes to the favor and blessings of God. Yes, God may allow you to face hardships, but it's all for your good to mature you in Christ. Some people will try to discourage you from aiming high in life because they feel it may cause you to lose focus on Christ and start craving things of the world. The Bible says: "We are in this world but not of this world" (John 15:19). This means that although we are physical beings in the world, we are not partakers of it, nor do we condone its values and standards.

Nevertheless, we can be just as, if not more, accomplished, ful-filled, and successful as those who are not in Christ. Do not let the world paint a picture to you that you can only go so far in being successful as a saved millennial. Matter of fact, you have an advantage of experiencing spiritual and natural blessings. You are more prone to excel than anyone else. Why? Because you have chosen to follow Christ. God will always take care of his own. Shadrach, Meshach, and Abednego were all young men working within the secular world who refused to bow to the king's image. Although they were thrown in the fiery furnace for not denouncing Christ, they were ultimately preserved and rescued by Jesus himself. This is a perfect example of how God will always come to your defense when you choose to follow him. There are no glass ceilings when you are in Christ. No good thing will be withheld from you. Don't make room for the enemy to disillusion you to believe otherwise. He is a pathetic deceiver.

David is another example of how far and high you can soar with Christ. He was anointed to be a king in his youth. God didn't wait until he was fully developed mentally or physically to give him his favor. Instead, he did it in David's most vulnerable years. Although his peers regarded him as just another young person, lacking maturity and responsibility, God esteemed him as the apple of his eye. Not only did he defeat giants, but he became king of Israel. Had he decided to put boundaries on his life, he would have never experienced the success he received both naturally and spiritually. You are a David, waiting to be unveiled to your generation. God has strategically placed you in a position that will bring glory to his name. As you see your life catapulting forward, pause and thank God for his favor and blessings.

Declaration: My winning capacity is not limited. I can do all things through Christ.

Prayer: God, I thank you because your love for me has no limits. Thank you for all the blessings you've bestowed upon me. I thank you that I will be successful in you. By faith, I will reject all thoughts that cause me to feel less than. I thank you for choosing me to live a life above the status quo. Help me to persevere as I go higher in you and tap into my unlimited potential. In Jesus's name, I pray. Amen.

DAY 10

Rocking My Favor

*For whoso findeth me findeth life and shall obtain
favor of Jehovah. (Proverbs 8:35)*

Have you ever stopped to consider why certain things happened to others around you but passed right by you? Perhaps you have witnessed someone work extremely hard to accomplish a goal when you accomplished the same goal almost effortlessly. You may have experienced difficulties that cost someone else their sanity, yet you rose above. Overcoming setbacks, disappointments, and failures that have consumed others is a strong indicator of the favor of God being on your life. Guess what? You can unapologetically walk in that favor. No explanations are needed. The sovereignty of God is unexplainable. Many people will question why favor rests on you. The Word of God tells us to delight ourselves in the Lord, and he will give us the desire of our heart (Psalm 37:4). So, God grants favor to those who learn to honor him. Everyone who appears to be prosperous and happy in life is not necessarily favored by God. And those with favor ought not to think they will avoid challenges, tests, and trials.

The Word of God provides examples of great men possessing favor, yet they still endured hardships. God's favor is on you because, while other millennials are living their lives based upon societal standards, you chose to adhere to the calling of Christ. Walk boldly in your favor. You will not have to compete with anyone to earn the favor of God. It's God's preferential treatment given to you. Please beware: along with favor may come a bigger responsibility or burden because you chose to follow Christ. However, do not allow this to discourage you. As you've been reminded countless times before, you are destined to overcome any obstacle designed to hinder you in your relationship with God. The spirit living down in the inside of you makes you more capable of handling the enemy's devices victoriously. What say ye? Are you ready to be a picture example of God's favor? All he requires is your yes! Get ready to be envied and admired.

Affirmation: The favor of God surrounds me. I cannot lose.

Prayer: Heavenly Father, you never cease to amaze me. You could have chosen anyone else to be an image of your glory. Thank you for the favor, blessings, and grace you have given me. Thank you for making my life a true testament of your faithfulness. Help me to embrace this favor with confidence and humility. In Jesus's name, I pray. Amen.

DAY 11

I'm on Display

Show yourself to be a model of good works,
and in your teaching show integrity, dignity.
(Titus 2:7)

To attract buyers, retailers often put their best pieces of work on display. Doing so drives consumers to inquire on certain products and, ultimately, patronize the merchandizer. Translation: You are on display for the kingdom of God. People will use your lifestyle and everything you stand for to determine if they will choose to live for Christ. Your life should be an example to others. Being on display for Christ means you will need to ensure your daily walk is not contrary to what it is you stand for. People expect Christians to be flawless, but we know that is impossible. Although we cannot be perfect, our lives can be a reflection of Godly principles and statues. Every aspect of our lives must reflect Christ. We cannot pick and choose which Christian values to uphold. We must yield ourselves completely to the Word of God.

It's impossible to be sold out for Christ without denying the things of the world. The world says, "Do you and whatever pleases you. Be not deceived. " This contradicts the Word of God. Luke 19:23 boldly proclaims, "If any man will come after me, let him deny himself." The world says, "If someone hates you, hate them back and cut them off." God says, "Love your enemies and do good to those who hate you" (Matthew 5:24). The world says, "Follow your heart when making life decisions." God says, "The heart is deceitful above all things and desperately wicked" (Jeremiah 17:9). So, in actuality, we need to be saved from our hearts. The world believes premarital sex is needed to fully connect with someone. The Word of God urges us to flee from fornication (1 Corinthians 6:18). Get the picture? God needs someone he can trust to be a model millennial who will boldly display kingdom values. Ready to rip the runway? This is no simple task, as your life will be under constant scrutiny. With the help of God, you can be that perfect example the world believes does not exist. Not only will you be on display for everyone to see your lifestyle, but you will be a living example of how favor looks. What message are you conveying to your peers? Do you stand out from the crowd? Are you committed to being a model for Christ? Is your conversation becoming to that of a Christian? Do you frequent places the world is known to be at? Does your lifestyle depict Christian values? These are just a few examples of the myriad questions that arise for someone on display. Let's vow to stay committed to the cause and avoid bringing open shame to Christ.

Declaration: I am committed to being a model for Christ.

Prayer: Lord, thank you for counting me worthy enough to represent you. I realize the call is great, but I'm committed to the charge. Thank you for using my life to attract others to you. Let my words and actions be a reflection of you at all times. I thank you that your grace will go before me and keep me. In Jesus's name, I pray. Amen.

DAY 12

Visible Faith

For I am not ashamed of the gospel: For it is the
power of God unto salvation to everyone that
believeth to the Jew first, and also to the Greek.
(Romans 1:16)

As believers of Christ, we are called to share the gospel with the world. Now that you have come into the realization of Christ, it's crucial to witness to others the truth about God's love. Visible faith simply means to exemplify your raining truth. What is it that you believe? Can others tell the difference from you and the nonbeliever? Not just by your testimony, but by your everyday actions. Other millennials need role models who represent the persona of who they aspire to become spiritually. It's important to not only articulate God's Word, but to be a reflection of it. Everything we do in life requires some level of faith. We live our lives based on the value system embedded in us by our parents or those who raised us. We are often put in positions that will challenge us to denounce our values and go against our moral convictions. Often we will choose to follow our convictions because we have been conditioned to be true ourselves.

However, there are times we choose not to follow the convictions of our teaching, and the end result bears repercussions. The Word of God admonishes us to live so that your life will bring others into the truth of Jesus Christ. You can't say you agree with the Word of God but refuse to display the attributes of Christ. Get excited about the good news. Show others your faith is so remarkable, that it needs to be shared with the world. The enemy will not see you as a threat to his kingdom if you are only professing your faith when no one is watching. What good is your faith if no one knows about it but you? Are your friends aware of your salvation? Do your friends consult you for spiritual advice? These are questions to ask yourself to determine if you visibly show your faith. Toting a Bible everywhere you go, praying openly on social media, and quoting Scriptures does not count as visibly reflecting your faith. These acts are not considered genuine, as they lack substance. Visible faith is backed by lifestyle. What are your conversations like? Who are you calling friend? Do you share the good news with others, or is your faith silent? We've already determined how great a call it is to live for Christ. Did you answer the call out of fear and intimidation, or did you answer out of faith? You are here to make an impact on your generation. It's time to live out loud!

Declaration: I will walk confidently in my faith.

Prayer: Dear God, I am not ashamed of you. I boldly declare you as the absolute God, and beside you, there is no other. Prepare me to be an effective witness to build your kingdom. Remove any feelings of shame or fear that may come from proclaiming your name. Let my testimony and daily walk draw others to you. Let your name be magnified forevermore. In Jesus's name, I pray. Amen.

DAY 13

The Heart of True Religion

Pure religion and undefiled before our God and
Father is this, to visit the fatherless and widows
in their affliction, and to keep oneself unspotted
from the world. (James 1:27)

There is a huge theory circulating that religion is manmade and not biblically supported. Wrong! In fact, strict protocol is given concerning religion, and to not accept religion is quite contrary to the charge God has placed upon us. As Christians, we are guilty of practicing certain traditions and customs and integrating these practices as religious acts mandated by God. Because these practices may appear to be stringent rules almost impossible for the modern Christian to exemplify, many Christians are prone to believe religion is manmade and not God's perfect will. So, essentially, we act and live according to our own personal convictions rather than seeking to please God. Yes, as Christians, we are just as responsible for corrupting the true meaning of religion as the world. No, we are not losing our religion, but we are holding fast to it.

Religion is a belief system or doctrine people choose to follow as it pertains to believing in a higher authority. As a Christian, our religion is based upon the belief that God sent his only begotten son, Jesus, to earth to redeem mankind. Thus, Christianity is birthed out of Christ. Therefore, by following Christ, one is considered a Christian.

The Bible has given us several examples of what being a Christian means in terms of how Christ lived while on earth and the decree he established for those choosing to follow him. The Word of God tells us that when Jesus wasn't feeding the hungry, healing the sick, and saving souls, he was going forth in ministry, preaching and teaching to the masses. He provided a great example of how we ought to be as Christians. You're not too young to do outreach, you're not too inexperienced to pray for the sick, and you're not too out of touch with Christ to witness to a non-believer. What better time than now to practice your religion? The time of impact is now! Christians have lost their impact because they have lost their religion. I dare you to dismiss every silly conundrum you've heard about Christianity. No other religion will have as much impact as we will. Untangle yourself from the web of deceit that the world has placed on religion, specifically Christianity. Be fearless! Grab hold of your religion, hang on to it, embrace it, live it, and most of all, share it.

Declaration: I will remain firm in my beliefs, never giving up my religion.

Prayer: Gracious Father, I thank you that your truth has been revealed to me. Help me to follow through in my walk as you intended. Today I choose to renew my commitment to you. Thank you for the revelation of what true religion is. Fix my thoughts concerning Christianity and help me to be the Christian this world needs to see. In Jesus's name, I pray. Amen.

DAY 14

"Ease on down the Road"

No temptation has overtaken you that is not common to man. God is faithful, and he will not let you be tempted beyond your ability, but with the temptation he will also provide the way of escape that you may be able to endure it. (1 Corinthians 10:13)

Hold up!! Wait!! Did someone say ease…on down the road? If you're thinking there's nothing easy about this road, you're absolutely correct. However, there is nothing about this road that hasn't been encountered by those who have taken it before you, even Christ himself. God already knows the road you will take, and he knows exactly what you will encounter along the way. He's familiar with every distraction, every naysayer, every struggle, and every obstacle the enemy will construct to detour and reroute you. Obstacles are attracted to people with purpose. Don't be alarmed of your surroundings, because God has already planned your victory. From the moment you totally yielded your life, he made a promise of providing a pathway to escape everything that was created to annihilate you. Doesn't it feel good to know there's perfect security in Jesus? Many Christians started on their journey, and when the road began to look different than how they perceived it would be, they ventured off. Following Christ will never be the popular thing to do among your peers. You will encounter people who will attempt to get you to renounce your faith. There will always be a group of people to challenge your beliefs, criticize your values, and make mockery of your lifestyle. Unfortunately, it's supposed to happen this way. Just stay on the road! Don't take offense and don't get discouraged. It's all part of the journey.

A popular poem written by Robert Frost, "The Road Not Taken," speaks about the road less traveled. This is also spoken of in the Word of God, where he points out the road leading to him is narrow, while the most popular road the world takes is wide (Matthew 7:14). The road to Christ is the road less traveled. As Christians following Christ, we chose to free ourselves from the conformity of the world, with the intentions of making an impact. Our hopes are that our trail will become the road more often traveled. When we follow the path Christ has set for us, we deviate from the norm and prove to the world just how powerful he is. Everyone following Christ will be tempted at some point while traveling on this road. But remember, victory will always be your outcome when you are in Christ. You will always triumph. You will never understand your wherewithal until you are tempted. God knows that you're capable of withstanding and will never put you in a place to be defeated. Keep easing on down the road. Soon you will arrive at your destination (destiny).

Declaration: I will overcome every obstacle set on my path with grace by faith.

Prayer: God, I thank you that you have made me victorious from the beginning. I thank you for the pathway of escape you've created for me. You've already overcome the world, so teach me to follow in your footsteps. Help me to continue on the path that will lead me to the divine destiny you have purposed for me. I know you know my end, and I pray I will learn to totally depend on you to make this journey successful. In Jesus's name, I pray. Amen!

DAY 15

Hello, Fear

For God has not given us the spirit of fear, but of
power and of love and of a sound mind.
(2 Timothy 1:7)

I ntimidation is a ploy of the enemy. He understands and
recognizes the power you possess whether you do or don't.
He's obsessed with your life. He feels that if he can find
tactics to scare you, then he will ultimately turn you away from
God. He intends to steal, kill, and destroy you. However, the
Word of God always admonishes us to fear not. When you har-
bor fear, it causes your thinking patterns to be reshaped. Fear
causes us to be apprehensive of following through on our assignment. You've got to realize the power you've been endowed
with. You cannot allow fear to keep you from being all God
has intended you to be. There is so much favor on your life, so
the enemy is jealous and wants to stop you at all costs. Harness
your power! Walk in boldness knowing that God's got your
back. We've already discussed the significant role you have in

the kingdom of God. By now, you should fully understand the devil will never cease terrorizing you until you back down. Take courage and do not back down. So many millennials need to see courage in the face of others.

Conquer your fears with prayer! Torment the enemy with your devotion and worship. Nothing puts the enemy to flight more than a bold follower of Christ. We all have done things we were afraid of initially, but we decided to ignore the voice telling us to stop pursuing our goals. Aren't you glad you did not heed that false thought? During this journey with Christ, you will hear and endure things that will make you lose heart. Always remember: if what you hear does not align with God's Word concerning you, they are lies from the enemy. Don't be compelled to give up. The power that you have is greater than any demonic force, scare tactic, and lie the enemy can conjure up. Look fear in the eye and proclaim, "I will not be held hostage by you." The call on your life is so great that all you have to do is speak what God has said about you. Let the enemy know he is not in control of your destiny. Push through and hold on. You've got this! You're an overcomer because of who your Father is. Hello, fear. I am not afraid of you.

Declaration: Today I choose to walk in power. I am not afraid.

Prayer: Heavenly Father, your love for me never ceases to amaze me. I am aware of the great power that lies within me because you have chosen me to be your child. Help me to overcome my fears and cling to your will for my life. I thank you for courage, boldness, and the audacity to be all I can be for your kingdom. I place my faith over fear, and I commit to fulfilling my assignment. In Jesus's name, I pray. Amen.

DAY 16

Balance It Out

Do not be excessively righteous and do not be overly wise. Why should you ruin yourself? (Ecclesiastes 7:16)

Doctors recommend a balanced diet of nutrients, fruits, and vegetables to ensure good health. Those committed to maintaining a healthy lifestyle are very likely to stick to their doctor's recommendations. As a Christian millennial, you have the responsibility to live a balanced spiritual lifestyle. Who said being saved was boring? Christ came to give us an abundant life, which means we can live it to the fullest, enjoying our freedom in Christ. We do have to be aware of the enemy trying to disguise certain things as being appropriate to partake in. We must be careful not to involve ourselves in activities that may cripple our witness. We must ask the Holy Spirit to help us discern truth from error, ungodliness from righteousness, and carnality from holiness. We must learn to master distinction, which will, by and large, allow us to live a balanced life according to the principles of God. The enemy will forever be there in hopes of deceiving you in your walk. When determining if an act is Godly or not, ask yourself, "Would God approve of this? How is this edifying my spiritual man? Is this an activity that should be associated with a Christian?" Remember, Paul said all things are lawful, but all things are not expedient (1 Corinthians 10:23). This means that although most things are permissible, they may not be constructive for the Christian millennial.

Remember, your life is on display every day. Your peers are observing you to determine the true power of Christ, so don't let them down. It's ok to have fun, hang with friends, and maintain a social life, but be aware that the enemy is not going to allow you to live in peace. He will always devise a plan to attack your character and your testimony. Balance is important! The Bible admonishes us not to be overly righteous. We must find that balance to please God in all of our ways while ensuring we are relatable enough to draw others to Christ. The world will always depict living a good life as doing whatever will make you happy. Remember, your fleshly desires will never align with kingdom values. Try to avoid receiving advice from those who are not rooted and stable in Christ. To avoid error, consult the Holy Spirit to lead you into truth and righteousness. The enemy will always justify why you can do things that you should avoid. Don't forget that he will never agree with the Word of God. Embrace God's recommendation for a balanced spiritual diet.

Declaration: I will maintain a balanced spiritual lifestyle.

Prayer: Dear God, help me to remain upright and steady. I trust that you will guide my footsteps along this path. Thank you for a healthy balance in my spiritual, social, professional, and personal life. I believe your Word over the word of the enemy. Allow my testimony to be effective and impactful to all those I come into contact with. In Jesus's name, I pray. Amen.

DAY 17

Walk It Out

Be not therefore anxious for the morrow: for the morrow will be anxious for itself. (Matthew 6:34)

The time will come when you will become weary of well-doing. There will be times you will feel overwhelmed and want to cancel your subscription with the kingdom. Everything worth having is worth the fight and tenacity to push through. Sometimes you will feel the pressure from your peers, world-influencers, etc. The pressure, at times, will bring you to a position of abandoning your journey with Christ. What you must understand is that your journey doesn't have to be completely mapped out. You do not have to be able to understand everything about the journey. Take it one day at a time. Walk your journey out step by step and day by day. No rush! You will never know in depth what God's plan is for your life, but you must trust his hand. Father knows best. He instructs us to take no thought of what will occur tomorrow or the next day or the next week.

Everything happens according to his perfect timing. He never asks us to understand his plan for our journey, but forever admonishes us to trust him.

Trusting God is not always easy, especially when we can't trace his hand on our lives. We sit in expectation at times for things to happen concerning us, and sometimes we walk away disappointed. Lace up your shoes and keep walking in your purpose. Sidetracked? Keep moving. Eventually God will confirm your next move. Stuck? Wiggle your way out of the spiritual quicksand and pick back up where you left off. The entire kingdom of God is rooting for you. The key to a successful life in Christ is to walk with him daily. That means one day at a time. Christ is our daily bread, which means we need a dose of him daily to maintain our Christian walk. We may have gotten discouraged yesterday, but today is a new day with an all-inclusive package of new mercy. Take it, use it, and keep moving. When you mess up, just remember you are not disqualified from the love of God. Repent, refocus, reposition, and move it along. Be grateful for his faithfulness and loving-kindness. Don't dwell on yesterday or what will occur tomorrow. God's Word confirms your steps are already ordered by him, and he delights in your way. Walk out your faith and prove to the enemy he will forever be defeated. His time is up!

Declaration: I will be persistent in my daily walk with Christ.

Prayer: Gracious Father, thank you for the strength to walk out my Christian walk daily. I pray that when I drift toward anxiety, your love will pull me back towards you. Help me to see the big picture and not dwell on the trivial things. I thank you for loading me with benefits all the days of my life. I will forever revere you. In Jesus's name, I pray. Amen.

DAY 18

Ethics 101

Seeing that his divine power hath granted unto us all things that pertain unto life and godliness, through the knowledge of him that called us by his own glory and virtue. (2 Peter 1:3)

W e've all, at some point, questioned whether certain characteristics of Christianity were man-made or God-ordained. As a Christian, your flesh will forever be at war with your spirit. God's will is for us to seek out his principles, which will enable us to live an ethical lifestyle. We've all had someone to challenge our belief system, especially when it comes to behavior that is deemed to be fun and constructive for millennials. Pious leaders are often heard quoting the dos and don'ts of the Word of God. Yes, there is definitely a list of things that we have been explicitly directed to refrain from, and there are things that can be done to show others the power of Christ, such as the familiar cliché of turning the other cheek. God never intended for this journey to be impossible to accomplish, but he did warn us of what comes with the territory of being a Christian.

The Bible does not give direct instructions on all situations we encounter in life, but the expectation is that you will search the heart and mind of Christ and follow the principles and standards by which the Holy Spirit directs us to abide by. Certain acts are not ethical according to the precepts of God. The Bible urges us to follow the authorities that God himself has put into place, so the opinions of the world concerning Christian ethics are irrelevant. If there are certain behaviors you believe are contrary to the principles of God, the best decision to make is to allow the Holy Spirit to guide you into truth. Your unsaved friends cannot decide how to live morally in the sight of God. The world will never be in agreement with spiritual concepts. Let's go back to the basics, Ethics 101, the Christian way.

Abandon those worldviews that attempt to lure you into living opposite of what God desires. Godly behavior directly contradicts the way the world operates. Christian ethics goes against the grain of society. Come out from among them and be ye separate saith the Lord (2 Corinthians 6:17).

Declaration: I will live boldly and without compromise according to God's Word.

Prayer: Thank you, God, for your Holy Spirit. You understood the struggle I would have on this journey from the beginning, and you chose to equip me beforehand. Your love for me runs deep. Help me to cherish your Word so that I may live according to it and not the world. Shift my focus and help me heed instruction from the Holy Spirit. In Jesus's name, I pray. Amen.

DAY 19

Glow in the Dark

Even so let your light shine before men, that they
may see your good works, and glorify your father
who is in heaven. (Matthew 5:16)

In a world where darkness (wickedness) is prevalent, God is calling on his people to shine through it. Devices that yield light are often used in situations where darkness abides. Candles are not used in places where light penetrates. Their sole purpose is to shine but for a moment or in a small space. The Word of God refers to Christ as being the light of the world. Why the analogy? Because there is no confusion in light, it is not hard to comprehend. Light speaks for itself, and it stands alone. Being a light will allow those who are seeking an answer to life to be led to that answer. It's time to rise up and glow in the dark. We cannot remain comfortable being surrounded by darkness. Christ did not save us to remain a secret. Your light should shine so brightly that it becomes contagious. Your testimony should be so strong that others become captivated and desire to know the God you serve. We are called to illuminate where there is darkness. The darkness of this world is attributed to sin. Where sin is prevalent, light does not abide. This epidemic is growing worse by the day.

When Christians lose to sin, the world suffers, and darkness occurs. We must glow in the dark to avoid a massive spiritual blackout. Your light must continue to shine even in the darkest places. Your light is not a clap-on, clap-off feature. You should be glowing in your community, workplace, friendships, and relationships. Everyone you come in contact with should encounter your glow. God is who kindles your light. God is who lights us up. After you have yielded to him and put away your own self-righteousness, then and only then can the Father endow us with the light of his love. The glow is real. Don't be afraid to glow out of fear of how others may perceive you. Remember, the world is watching you. Be the difference. Be the example! Be what the world feels doesn't exist. Love God so much that it spills over into the lives of sinners. Only when they experience our light will darkness dispel.

Declaration: I will allow my light to penetrate through a world of darkness.

Prayer: Heavenly Father, I pray that in a world of wickedness and darkness, you will cause me to stand out. I pray my glow will attract others to the kingdom. Let your glory shine through me. Help me to never forget the reason for this high calling. Thank you for selecting me to be a reflection of you. I pray to forever make you proud to call me your child. In Jesus's name, I pray. Amen.

DAY 20

Hungry? Why Wait?

Blessed are they that hunger and thirst after righteousness for they shall be filled.
(Matthew 5:6)

You are what you eat! How many times have we heard this phrase? Health experts often use this statement to compel us to be mindful of the foods we consume. So, if you consume healthy foods, chances are you'll be healthy, and if you consume unhealthy foods, chances are you will be unhealthy. A healthy diet increases your chance of longevity. Now we understand that not only do nutritionists set standards for healthy living, but so does Christ. That's right; Christ wants us to be mindful of our spiritual diet. What have you consumed lately? Who's on your playlist? Who are you calling friend? What books are you reading? What does your spiritual diet consist of? What does your appetite crave? What are you hungry for?

Christ is calling for millennials to hunger after righteousness. That means you should crave to be righteous in all your conduct. Have a desire to be fulfilled by the things of God. We can choose to have an earthly role model or mentor; however, Christ will forever be the perfect example for us. He requires us to be holy. Yes, millennials are called to holiness as well. The spirit of Christ within you enables you to live a more righteous life. Don't ignore the convictions of the spirit. Its purpose is to lead you into all truth and righteousness. If you feed the spiritual man, it will grow, develop, and mature. Eventually you won't be bogged down with the same temptations. The spirit will always guide you to a place of safety in Christ. Let it lead you! Overcome the temptation to resort back to sin and iniquity. Feed your spiritual man daily. Don't let him starve. Even if you are not hungry, force-feed yourself the Word of God. Get in his presence and remain there. Allow your hunger for Christ to be so strong that others will become hungry from watching you. Become so desperate for Christ that nothing else matters. Remember, if you seek his righteousness more than anything and before anything, he will add to you everything else you need. Recess is over! The way in is Christ. The way is through Christ. The way over is Christ. Fuel your hunger with the Word, fasting, prayer, meditation, service, and worship. This is a recipe for a healthy spiritual lifestyle.

Hungry? Why wait?

Declaration: I will feed my spiritual man daily to grow stronger in Christ.

Prayer: God, here I am again. Help me to be mindful of my spiritual intake. I am aware of what it takes to please you. Help me to be righteous. Remove any desire that exalts itself against your righteousness. Help me starve my fleshly desires. Extract the residue of sin and iniquity in my life and continue to let your spirit guide me into truth. In Jesus's name, I pray. Amen.

DAY 21

Eyes Wide Shut

And he said, Go, and tell this people, Hear ye
indeed, but understand not, and see ye indeed
but perceive not. (Isaiah 6:9)

On our spiritual journey we must understand everything is not meant for the Christian to hear, see or
partake in. Social media has a great impact on society, especially on the young. It is easy to see things that are
not meant for our spiritual man to bear witness to. We cannot
control what is allowed to circulate in the atmosphere. After
all, the Bible tells us the enemy is prince of the power of the
air (Ephesians 2:2). That's right: God granted Satan power over
the earthly realm. However, he's designated as a prince because
there is only one king – Jesus. Satan has the power to manifest
wickedness by influencing people. But remember, his power is
limited. Since we are in the world but not of the world, we must
be on guard at all times to avoid falling for the enemy's tricks.
We must learn to discern when the enemy is trying to deceive
us. Our eyes must be open to see what is going on in the world,

but our spiritual eyes must understand when they must be shut to avoid Satan's tactics.

We will always hear things that are not spiritually sound or biblically supported. The world will always have their version of what a Christian should be. The world is bold enough to have leaders in high places teach doctrines and introduce ideologies not aligned with the Word of God. Listen to what is being said but do not attempt to comprehend foolishness. Guard your eyes and ears. If you hear something that does not connect with your spiritual man, do not accept it into your spirit. Part of the job of the Holy Spirit is to guide you into truth. If truth is not being spoken, your spiritual alarm will sound off, confirming your inclinations. It's important to keep your eyes open and not closed. You must be able to see and hear so that you understand the pattern of the enemy and know which spiritual strategy to use to combat him. It will take time, but eventually it will become easier to detect the enemy's schemes. Remain vigilant and conscious of your surroundings. Don't allow things you see and hear in the world to shape your spiritual viewpoint. Keep your eyes wide shut.

Declaration: I will remain focused at all costs to avoid the enemy's ploys.

Prayer: Lord, I thank you for my sight. I thank you for ears to hear and feelings to feel. I thank you that, although I am a natural being, you've given me spiritual capabilities to detect the enemy. I pray that I will not be moved or distracted by what the world displays, but will stand confidently and securely on your Word. I pray that your voice will always be the loudest voice I hear. In Jesus's name, I pray. Amen.

DAY 22

Fighting Temptations

There hath no temptation taken you but such as
is common to man: but God is faithful, who will
not suffer you to be tempted above that ye are
able; but will with the temptation also make a
way to escape, that ye may be able to bear it.
(1 Corinthians 10:13)

Temptations arise to test our discipline and commitment to Christ. Jesus himself was tempted by Satan to make him abandon his purpose, which would leave humanity doomed to eternal damnation. Jesus understood how important it was to fight and overcome temptation. Satan attempted to bargain with Jesus. However, Jesus refused to submit to temptation because he knew humanity's right to salvation was centered around him overcoming the temptations of Satan. Satan aims to mislead you and sabotage your relationship with Christ. He comes to tempt you in all areas of your life, mentally, physically, intellectually, and spiritually. If he can't attack you in one area, he will move to the next. Temptations cover a broad spectrum. We automatically associate temptation with physical lust; however, it encompasses materialism, pride, and egoism.

Your ego will convince you to believe you are strong in areas you are weak in. To overcome temptation, you must practice discipline. We must set boundaries and stick to them. We cannot allow our fleshly desire to prevail over righteousness. We must be accountable as well as watch and pray, knowing the enemy is on a continuous prowl for Christians who will denounce Christ. We must fight temptations with spiritual tools. Self-discipline is a great tool, but we are wrestling with spiritual wickedness, which means we must also use spiritual tools to fight temptation. We cannot use worldly tactics and expect to win the battle over sinful nature. Our desires must align with what God desires. We must practice behaving justly to build discipline and character.

Every Christian face temptation. The enemy knows your weak points and just how to seduce you. Because you are tempted does not mean Christ does not dwell in you. Even Jesus was tempted. Temptation can lead to sin, but you determine if it will. You can combat the urge to sin by prayer. Prayer reroutes all things contrary to the knowledge of Christ. If you know certain actions will draw you further from Christ, such as partying, drinking, social media, or being around unsaved friends, take preventative measures to avoid these temptations. Put your dukes up. It's time to fight!

Declaration: My mind, body, and spirit will be subject to the leading of the Holy Spirit.

Prayer: God, please let my heart be receptive to the leading of the Holy Spirit. Help my desires become Godly desires. Temptation is absolutely everywhere. Grant me the strength to overcome temptations just as you have. Help me yield to you and protect me from me. In Jesus's name, I pray. Amen.

DAY 23

Law of Attraction

Finally brethren, whatsoever things are pure,
whatsoever things are honorable, whatsoever
things are of good report, if there be any virtue,
and if there be any praise, think on these things.
(Philippians 4:8)

The law of attraction teaches us that focusing on positive or negative thoughts dictates the experiences one will have in their lifetime. The thought is that if you exude positive energy, you will attract the same energy, which has an impact on your overall well-being. However, the same can be said for negative energy. The law of attraction is not biblically supported per se, but there are many scriptural references congruent with this thought process. The Word of God provides examples of individuals who changed the trajectory of their lives through the way they chose to think and function. God is calling you to operate on a different level. You cannot afford to have a distorted concept of who God wants you to be. Take a look in your spiritual mirror to see what your reflection yields.

Who's attaching themselves to you? What spiritual barriers can you just not seem to overcome? These are definitive questions to pose when examining your Christian walk.

Are you focusing on things that are guaranteed to keep you close to God? What you focus on the most will be what governs your life. God does not want anything to come before him. We cannot allow the enemy room to creep in. He slips in through our thoughts, so if your focus remains on Christ, the enemy will have a difficult time manipulating you. Many Christian millennials are burdened with depression because their focus and energy are on things they see with their natural eye. There will always be a spiritual battle with the enemy over your life. You must remain steadfast! You must consider the things that will attract you to Christ as well as the things that will drive us apart from him. Your spiritual image should be a reflection of Christ. When this happens, you will attract all of the kingdom's blessings because Christ will honor your submission and obedience.

Declaration: I commit to changing my thinking to change the trajectory of my life.

Prayer: Dear God, I humbly submit my thought process to you so that I am in alignment with spiritual concepts. Help my thoughts, ways, and actions to be a split image of you. Help me to be able to attract other millennials by projecting and living life according to the spiritual values you have set for me. In Jesus's name, I pray. Amen.

DAY 24

Chasing God's Heart

*But seek first his kingdom and his righteousness
and all other things will be given to you as well.
(Matthew 6:33)*

After chasing success, fame, wealth, status, power, etc.,
nothing is more gratifying than God. Whether we
choose to admit it or not, what we do in life is strongly motivated by our hearts. What we love and value determines
how we live our lives. Be careful of the things you love. God's
Word tells us the heart is deceitful and desperately wicked. This
means we must be attentive to the heart of God and not our
own hearts. Choosing the heart of God requires us to seek after
all things kingdom related. Remember, your life has brand-new
meaning now that you've decided to live for Christ. Chasing
the heart of God involves allowing him to develop us into vessels of honor. We must be changed, filled with his spirit, and
maintain an active relationship with him.

It's in quiet and alone time with God that he will unveil his heart
to you. By nature, we are self-seeking rather than God-seeking.

If we want to be youths after God's own heart, we must consistently spend quality time in his presence and in devotion. You cannot grow in the things of God unless you get to know the heart of God and spend time with him. God reveals himself through his Word. You must incorporate reading his Word so that he will show you his heart. As you become more in tune through daily devotion, your heart will begin to develop and grow. The Bible tells us that David was a man after God's own heart. This statement has always propelled readers to consider why such a high affirmation was given to David. Through all of David's life, beginning from youth, he understood the importance of seeking the heart of God. He was the epitome of a God-chaser.

Often we seek the hand of God and all the perks and benefits that come with being his child, but we do not seek his heart. Ask him to show you what he requires of you. Ask him to remove traits that would cause you to be a stumbling block to your peers. Ask for the courage to be bold and dauntless. Now is the time to rise up and become what God is beckoning us to become: the embodiment of love and grace. Consider the things you are actively pursuing in your life, whether they pertain to your personal, spiritual, educational, or relational goals. Anything you are in pursuit of requires your dedication, time, energy, and commitment. Choose today to fully surrender your will to pursue the heart of God and to allow his heartbeat to get even louder on earth.

Declaration: I submit my heart, mind, and will to pursuing the heart of God.

Prayer: Heavenly Father, forgive me for the times I asked for what was in your hand and never asked for your heart. I admit I have been selfish and asking things amiss. I desire to please you and make you proud to call me your child. God, I ask that you intensify my pursuit of you. As the deer pants after the brook, my soul longs for you. Help me to seek the kingdom, knowing that you will reward me with the desires of my heart if I put you before anything else. I turn over my will in exchange for yours. Thank you for drawing me closer to you. In Jesus's name, I pray. Amen!

DAY 25

The Prayer Closet

And he spake a parable unto them to the end that
they ought always to pray, and not to faint.
(Luke 18:1)

Before the movie *War Room* became a hit phenomenon, the prayer closet was where people retreated to when they needed an intimate encounter with God. The prayer closet was not a physical place, but a spiritual safe haven that allowed you direct access to God without the background noise. The prayer closet was more than just a place of solitude to talk to God; it was a place to strengthen yourself, re-shift, re-focus, and, most of all, have intimacy with God. Prayer is conversation with God. It is the way we verbally communicate with the man who knows us better than we know ourselves. Prayer allows us to be our most vulnerable selves. It allows us to pour our issues, problems, insecurities, complexes, and anything we face onto the feet of God. In return, he will pour out his mercy, grace, love, favor, and anything else that he recognizes we need to sustain us. A relationship with God cannot be strengthened without a consistent prayer life.

The most important component of any relationship is communication. Communication is the foundation on which strong relationships are sustained. The beginnings of most personal relationships are centered around getting to know that individual and them getting to know you. No matter how much you have heard about them or know of them, it does not compare to you discovering who they are for yourself. When establishing a relationship, whether be it business or personal, it's important to not allow what you've heard about an individual to interfere with how you embrace or perceive them. God has a reputation for being the most faithful friend of all. When you think of the word "closet," you instantly think of a place where items are stored. You think of an enclosed space that allows you to put things away until time of use. You can look at the prayer closet the same way. You can store your worship, praise, devotion, and so much more in a safe place where you will be able to access them anytime you need them. God propels us to pray without cease because he knows that when we are prayed up, the enemy will have a hard time distracting or deceiving us.

Prayer is one of the main components to strengthening your walk with Christ. You can never learn the true essence of who God is unless you communicate with him on a consistent basis. There are no specific guidelines on what to say in prayer. All

God asks is that you talk to him. Your prayers do not have to be long, extravagant, and full of difficult words, but pure, heartfelt, and sincere. Those are the prayers that God honors. The more you talk to God, the stronger you will become. Spending time with him tells him just how important he is to you, and you'll find out just how important you are to him. As a result of your commitment to him, he will favor you and bless you beyond your imagination. At times, you will be so consumed with everyday life that it will seem almost impossible to keep a prayer life, but just as we make time to do things we desire to do, we must put the same effort in making ourselves available to talk to God. Don't allow life to interfere with your relationship with God.

Declaration: I commit to staying connected to God through a constant prayer life.

Prayer: God, I thank you for drawing me close to you. I realize how important prayer is in making this journey a success. God, I open my heart, ears, and spiritual eyes to the wisdom of your spirit. Help me to be established in word and prayer so that I may be guided into the destiny, purpose, and call you have for me. My aim is that I will go deeper in you and learn of you and make you proud to call me your child. You are what my soul desires. Help me to forever be focused on pleasing you in all I do. In Jesus's name, I pray. Amen.

DAY 26

Got Milk?

Like newborn babes crave pure spiritual milk, so
that by it you may grow up in your salvation.
(1 Peter 2:2)

Ilk is said to help develop strong bones. Calcium is an important mineral that our body needs to prevent our bones from fractures or breaking. There are many ways we can consume calcium. Drinking milk has always been the most preferable way to increase your calcium intake. For Christians, our spiritual milk is the Word of God. Just as calcium helps to strengthen our physical bones, the Word of God allows us to grow and mature in our relationship with Christ. Just as physical growth is essential for babies, spiritual growth is absolutely necessary for every believer. The Word of God is a critical component to Christian millennial success as it is with any other demographic. The same Word that brought us to life sustains us each day. Yes, we are saved now, but we are constantly growing all the time into a full and final salvation. We must nurture the Word of God just as newborn babes nurture their milk daily and consistently. There are plenty of other reading materials that will tempt us to indulge and distract us from reading the Word of God. We must remain alert as these schemes are set to stagnate our development in Christ.

Living the Christian life is not a mechanical process, but rather organic and progressive. Time spent with the Lord, in his presence, meditating on his Word, will allow us to be transformed into his likeness, thus making our spiritual journey successful. There are various reasons we need the Word of God. Not only does it allow us to understand the fullness of who God is, but it allows us to guard ourselves against false teachings about the Word. The Word of God advises us to be cautious of false teachers who prey on those who have no understanding of it. When the Word of God is within you, the spirit will alert you when you hear teaching that is contrary to what the Word has revealed. The world will forever have its opinion when it comes to the Word of God. We must not fall victim to erroneous teachings when it comes to what Christ requires of us. The Word of God will also prick our hearts once we become too comfortable. We have to make sure Christ is always first. We tread on dangerous ground when we drift from him and begin to do things our away against the Word. The Bible contains the mind of Christ. You cannot know the mind of Christ without his Word. The Word of God is active and alive, and those who hear it, read it, study it, and meditate on it tend to have the most stable relationship with God. Reading the Word should not be done just because it's something that God asks of you. We must get to the point in our journey where his word becomes an addiction, a habit, a consistent factor in our everyday lives. We should read his Word because we want to and it's good for us spiritually. This milk will alleviate malnourishment of our spiritual man. Before you read the Word of God, ask the Holy Spirit to speak to you through his Word. Remember, his Word is spirit and life.

Declaration: I will allow the Word of God to fill my memory and my heart and guide my footsteps.

Prayer: God, thank you for your Word. I realize your Word is one of the greatest sources of spiritual food. Help me to always crave your Word. I thank you for your Word, which encourages, convicts, defends, enlightens, restores, and transforms. Help me make room for your Word in my everyday life. Keep me from drifting away and saturate my heart with your Word. Lord, I vow to read your Word thoroughly to see the bigger picture. I thank you for your Word because it is true and holy, and your precepts are forever binding. Help me to fall in love with your Word so that I can keep my focus and live abundantly, just as you have destined me to live. In Jesus's name, I pray. Amen!

DAY 27

I Got This

I can do all things through Christ that strengthens me. (Philippians 4:13)

There will be times in our Christian walk where life will throw us curveballs testing our faith and belief in God. There will be great trials to challenge everything you know to be true about God. Challenges will attempt to overtake you, but they can never destroy you. With God, you have the wherewithal to withstand tough times in the face of adversity. God has enabled you, through the Holy Spirit, to live a victorious life. That means everything you set your heart and mind to do, you can accomplish. If walking with Christ seems to become a struggle more than a joy, you can rest assured that God will always give you the strength and courage to keep moving forward. God strengthens us beyond the good times and the "things are going good" moments. You can do all things through Christ, which means that you are not limited in any area of your life. You are the victor at all times. You possess the power to do all things, anything and everything, through the name of Christ.

One might ask, "Can I only do all things through Christ alone?" As a Christian, we must recognize the grace God grants us to live day by day. Without his grace, we can do nothing. We may see others thrive who may not even have a relationship with Christ, and this will cause us to question if we can do things on our own and still maintain a successful life. Keep this in mind: when we acknowledge God in every area of our life, he blesses us abundantly. God's glory is best seen as shining through us. The adversary will always make the lives of others seem to be blissful, but that is a deceptive tactic used to turn you away from God. Neglect these feelings, as they are not of God. The Holy Spirit not only strengthens us during tough times, but it helps us to grow through tough times. The Word of God commands us to put on the whole armor of God so that we may be able to withstand tough times (Ephesians 6:13). God already knew what we were up against. He knew we would feel helpless during difficult times. He knew that for you to truly know him, you would need situations to occur that made you rely totally on him to endure. The best part of the situation is that it has already been foreseen that you will be victorious through every trial. Doing all things through Christ can easily be interpreted as being able to acquire materialistic things by working extremely hard and putting God first. This is often the misconception many Christians have regarding this verse.

Although God's plan is for us to have an abundant life, this does not mean we will be exempt from pain, suffering, and life's disappointments. It does, however, mean that when you are tried by the enemy and provoked to losing hope, you will listen to the calming of the Holy Spirit encouraging you to press through the rough times, for with Christ, you will be able to persevere. You will get frustrated, you will get distracted, you will be challenged, and you will want to throw in the towel. All believers have, at some point in their journey, felt these emotions. The key is allowing God's voice to become the loudest voice you hear. You can endure, and you will be victorious. You are more than a conqueror. You can accomplish all things through Christ.

Declaration: Through Christ, I will continue to live a victorious life.

Prayer: God, it's evident that your love for me runs deep. Thank you for the grace to continue to tackle every hardship, trial, and difficulty in life. Thank you for empowering me to stay steadfast in my faith. Teach me to be solely dependent on your spirit and to reject every thought that whispers defeat in my ear. Teach me to harken to your voice for strength and encouragement. Help me to never choose my own voice over yours. I believe you have placed in me the power to win in every area of my life. Thank you for causing me to triumph. May you get the glory out of every win. In Jesus's name, I pray. Amen!

DAY 28

Access Granted

Behold, I have given you authority to tread on
serpents and scorpions, and over all the power of
the enemy, and nothing shall hurt you.
(Luke 10:19)

A traffic control officer has the power and authority to stop, start, and adjust traffic as he desires because he is backed by all branches of government. If one should choose to resist the power and authority of this officer, they would be subject to major repercussions. God has granted the believer power (the ability) and authority (legal right) to take dominion over both the spiritual and earthly realms. Even as a youth, you are capable of controlling what you allow to occur in your life. Often we may feel helpless in certain situations and believe things must remain how they are. Why so? God has given us access to dethrone any spirit or demonic force that tries to overtake us, our family, or friends. You are a force to be reckoned with. Believe it or not, but the enemy is afraid of you. You can stop his assignment to kill, steal, and destroy.

Take spiritual legal ownership of your territory. Don't bow out gracefully but put up a fight and show him the power that you possess. Most Christians never fully utilize their power and authority because the enemy has gripped them with fear. Did you know you have the capability of saving your generation? Did you know a family member can be cured according to the power that lies within you? Did you know the enemy must back down when you walk in power and authority? Just as the traffic cop is backed by branches of governmental power, heaven backs up your demand when you operate in your power and authority. You have full access to manipulate situations to work for your good. To gain access to something, you must have the proper code. Bankers cannot access the bank vault until they have successfully entered the correct code. What grants them access to the code is being fully mandated through training and being granted the ability (power) and legal right (authority) to conduct business on behalf of that entity.

When you were born again and received the Holy Spirit, you were endowed with the key code, and your access to the power of Christ was granted. Do not ever doubt the power you possess. You have the DNA of Christ, and even greater works will you be able to do. It's time to live out who we truly are. When we place our lives under God's protection, the enemy has no rule over us. God's power within us helps us to ward off the enemy. The enemy wants you to believe that, as a young person, you are inexperienced and unable to put the enemy in his place, but as always, he uses this deception to trick you. As previously discussed, you must be bold. This war we are waging on the enemy is fought daily. Each day, month, year, and season will bring a different degree of Satan's ploys. Don't yield. Stand on guard and resist him at all costs. Resist his words, his tricks, and his schemes. Let your boldness and courage in Christ be your resounding position. Your access to the kingdom has been fully granted.

Declaration: I take dominion over the enemy's territory and loose the peace of God for everyone and everything attached to me.

Prayer: God, I thank you for giving me governing power and authority over the enemy. Your word says that whatever I bind on earth shall be bound in heaven and the things I loose on earth shall be loosed in heaven. I bind confusion and loose peace of mind. Lord, help me to fully operate in my authority. I bind the spirit of fear and loose boldness and faith over my life. Help me to become all that you have called me. I take authority over my mind, body, and heart. I take authority over every troubling circumstance that makes me doubt your power. I take authority over the plan of the enemy to make me stagger and lose hope. I acknowledge the power of Christ in my life. In Jesus's name, I pray. Amen.

DAY 29

Church Juice

Not forsaking our own assembling together, as the
custom of some, but exhorting one another; and
so much more, as ye see the day drawing nigh.
(Hebrews 10:25)

Believe it or not, going to church is vital for every Christian believer. Churches are our spiritual pit stops, where you go to be replenished, restored, and encouraged and to be amongst other believers. Church is an essential part of your growth as a believer. A popular statement that can be heard today is: "You don't need to go to church; you are the church." This statement is why so many Christians choose not to attend church. Although I understand what is meant to be conveyed, it gives a false belief that attending church is not needed or required. This notion is deceptive, hence, the scripture mentioned above.

As a Christian millennial, you will be constantly bombarded with the views of society as they pertain to attending church. God has created an institution where you can come to dwell with like-minded individuals who will be able to recharge you for your spiritual journey. Yes watching your favorite preacher's podcasts, reading spiritual books, and listening to Christian music are all effective ways to help you on your spiritual journey, but they cannot take the place of assembling with believers. This is a pattern set by Christ since the beginning of time. It is a biblical practice to be kept throughout time. Going to church plays a major part in cultivating the skills, talents, and abilities God has placed in you. The world cannot cultivate your spiritual gifts. Do not reduce church to just a place where people go. It is God's house. It's a community; it's praising and worshipping with others. It's praying for others, watching others develop and mature. It's sharing in the trials and triumphs in the lives of others. It's making an impact and serving others. One reason we should attend church is that God requires it.

The Bible refers to the church as the bride of Christ. God expects us to love the things he loves and to keep his laws and precepts with all diligence. You must obey him even when we don't understand all that he requires. We must ask him to open up our understanding and plant the desire to fulfill what he would have us do. All of us long for a connection with others. It's our human nature to want to feel a sense of belonging. This connection can be acquired through gathering at church. It fulfills that desire within us to go through life with others. It's important to have a community of people who share the same values, beliefs, and faith as you. It makes your walk as a

Christian millennial easier when you are embraced and loved by your own. Each previous devotional has shed some light on practices to make your spiritual journey successful. This knits all of them together. Prayer, reading the word, and attending church regularly are key components to a successful Christian life. Don't allow the world to influence your walk with Christ. Go to church; don't stay home with the belief that you are better off. The church is where you will be refueled after the wear and tear of your daily walk. Press and assemble yourself where God dwells. Go get some church juice.

Declaration: God, I will dwell in your house all the days of my life.

Prayer: Lord, I thank you for creating an atmosphere where I can dwell amongst other believers. Teach me how to love the things you love. Help me to not focus on what the world says about fellowship. I trust that what you have set in order is what's best for my Christian journey. Lord, I commit to dedicating my time to coming together with my brothers and sisters in Christ to be a blessing to them as they are a blessing to me. Help me to never make excuses not to come to your house. I will enter into your gates with thanksgiving and enter into your courts with praise. In Jesus's name, I pray. Amen.

What Are You Talking About?

*Let no corrupt communication proceed out of
your mouth, but that which is good to the use
of edifying, that it may minister grace unto the
hearers. (Ephesians 4:29)*

A s a Christian, it is obvious that you must be mindful of what you say. The language you use should be
a reflection of what you stand for. One familiar saying is "If you don't have anything good to say, then don't say
anything at all." This saying holds true to this day. Often we
can get carried away and use language that is not befitting to
who we are in Christ. This is just not a reference to profanity;
any speech that does not edify, encourage, inspire, or give hope
should not be part of your language as a Christian. Society has
placed strong emphasis on how important it is for you to speak
your mind and say how you feel at all times… even if it brings
conflict. Freedom of speech is the most quoted amendment of
all. You have to remember that although it may be lawfully and
strongly encouraged, as a Christian the Word of God should

always be our compass when it comes to navigating the dos and don'ts of life.

Although using ungodly language may be a fad and the popular thing to do in our culture, always remember there are guiding principles as a Christian millennial that we must adhere to for our light to shine and stand apart from the world. Our culture says it's ok for women to be empowered and to express themselves, setting the bar for other women to follow suit. Men who use aggressive language are often viewed as dominant and no-nonsense guys who demand respect from others. Truth is, the language you use shows your level of maturity and wisdom. The Bible urges you to be mindful of not just how you live amongst non-believers, but how you talk. You cannot profess to be a follower of Christ using ungodly language. Of course, we have all at some point in our lives adapted a communication style that we use daily. In that case, it may be challenging to shift the language we are accustomed to using, but small steps can get us there. Watching your language is all-encompassing, which means you can choose not to use profanity but hold conversations filled with envy, jealousy, or even unbelief or doubt. This language can hurt you far more than any curse word can.

According to Proverbs 23:7, words, believe it or not, shape our thinking and can be a determining factor in our everyday lives. When you speak language contrary to kingdom language, you are forfeiting God's promises. Words can build us up or tear us down. As Christians, it's important to consider carefully the effect of our words, especially when we are frustrated, angry, or caught off guard. Sometimes we need to stop and ask ourselves, "Is it the proper thing to say this kind of joke or use these kinds of words?" You must ask yourself, "Will this cripple my witness as a representative for Christ?" We have to be mindful of the influence we have on those around us, especially those we have ministered to. If you are in Christ and have been filled with his spirit, your heart will be convicted when you have certain conversations that do not align with your Godly values. Even an unbeliever's conscience will be aroused when they go against the grain of their teachings. Many unindoctrinated people will often say the Bible does not condemn profanity, swearing, or such. Please know this is a false statement that further encourages the believer to feel they have the right to say what they want to say and how they want to say it. Refer to our focus scripture, which gives us a concrete command to avoid any corrupt speech. Do not allow the mass media to deceive you into believing that "freedom of speech" applies to you as a believer. It may be legal, but that does not make it acceptable to God. Practice incorporating words of love, affirmation, and positivity. As you practice daily, it will become a mindset, and you will see the beauty of Godly language.

Declaration: I choose to adopt the love language of Christ.

Prayer: Dear God, I admit that I am a work in progress. I realize that the words I say have a great impact on the lives of others around me. Help me never to forget your precepts. Help my speech to always show proper respect for you and all that is holy. Use my lips to strengthen, encourage, lift, and inspire all whom I come in contact with. Tame my tongue. Teach me self-control. Help me to keep a calm disposition so that I can avoid using language unbecoming to a Christian. I give you full control of my mouth. Help my speech to never hinder my influence for Christ. In Jesus's name, I pray. Amen!

DAY 31

Unfiltered Praise

Praise him for his mighty acts: Praise him according to his excellent greatness. (Psalm 150:2)

One of the greatest things we could ever do as a Christian is praise our God. Outside of prayer, we can read and obey his Word. He sets an expectation of praise. Praise tells God he is ruler and reigns supreme over any other thing. Praise is not just an emotional feeling that we display through singing, clapping, dancing, etc., but it is best demonstrated through sincere reverence and adoration. Praise allows God to manifest himself in our lives. There are so many things we have to praise God for, and as a Christian, we realize the power in giving him honor. The Bible shows us the true power of praise manifested in the lives of others. When we have a heart of praise, we are most vulnerable to the Holy Spirit. Praise unleashes life-changing miracles, torments the enemy, and draws us closer to God.

Although this often sounds like an easy task, the reality is that there will be times where our daily struggles or constant life demands dictate how we give praise to God. At times, praising God will seem more of a sacrifice than a joy. There will be times life just happens and gets the best of us and robs us of our praise, but here's what can make a lasting difference: praise him through the struggle. The sooner we decide to keep our eyes fixed on God and praise him no matter what's staring us in the face, the sooner we will suddenly realize that God's power has already released the grip those struggles appear to have over us. We must acknowledge he is God at all times and that he alone is worthy of our praise. There's power in your praise. Praise shifts the focus onto God. Society has strongly taught this generation how important "self" is. We need to be constantly reminded our purpose is not to praise ourselves but to put the attention on Christ, as he is deserving of all praise. We must be careful not to praise things or people, because God will not allow us to serve him and share his praise with anything/anyone else. The benefits of praise work both ways. Not only do you bless God when you praise, but God blesses you for your obedience to the command of praise. He refreshes and renews us when we praise him. His spirit will lift you up when you're down, strengthen you when you are weary, and give you peace amid chaos. There should never be a motive behind glorifying God.

Often we mistakenly identify praise as an act of singing, clapping, and dancing. These are outward acts of praise; however, they do not depict in whole what honoring God is. God's purpose of praise is to diminish the works of darkness, disinherit the enemy, and declare how powerful God is. Just as soldiers use specific weapons in battle to ward off the enemy, Christ has given us spiritual weapons to destroy our enemy. Along with several other weapons, such as prayer, the Word of God, fasting, and attending church, praise is a weapon that can be used for spiritual warfare. As you go forth in praise, the atmosphere around you will shift because you are operating in a foreign realm that the enemy cannot inhabit. Praise drives out the enemy. We are commanded to praise God according to Psalm 150:6. Praise is a call to thanksgiving, adoration, and submission. He is worthy of all of our gratitude. When we trust in the goodness of Christ, we will forever have a reason to give him the praise due to him. Praise shifts your focus, changes your attitude and perspective, and has the power to change the trajectory of our lives. We must learn to prioritize praise over complaining, praise over frustration, praise over discouragement, praise over pity, and praise over anything that sabotages our peace. God's plan for us is to prosper in all areas of our lives. We must maintain an attitude of gratitude, for this will make all the world of difference.

Declaration: Your praise will forever rest on my lips.

Prayer: Dear God, I praise you today with my whole heart. Hear my heart's song. I praise you for your faithfulness, never-failing love, and redeeming power. I confess my need and desire for you. I realize my life doesn't go so well when praise is not present. I struggle and worry, get weary and worn. Yet you never leave me. Thank you for your presence. Thank you for your care over me. Thank you for breathing renewal right into my soul. I pray that I will utilize a method of praise when I feel lost, confused, and cast down. I will make room for your spirit to work your purpose through me as I keep my eyes on you. In Jesus's name, I pray. Amen!

Acknowledgments

I must first thank my heavenly father, for, without God, I am the sum total of nothing. Thank you for choosing me to be a voice to my generation.

My completion of this project could not have been accomplished without November Media Publishing/Consulting. You guys are amazing and godsent. All I knew was that God had a message to be released to this generation and I was unsure of how to produce it. You took *The Kingdom Playlist* and turned it into something I never envisioned it would become. I appreciate you.

Finally, to one of the most incredible men to grace my life, my fiancé, Daniel Franklin II, my lead motivator, pusher, and faith stretcher. You've awakened the best parts of me, and I'm no longer afraid of the dark because you helped me discover my light. Thank you for being the real deal and for giving me permission to do the same.

CPSIA information can be obtained
at www.ICGtesting.com
Printed in the USA
LVHW081212121119
637079LV00012B/375/P